The editors would like to thank
BARBARA KIEFER, Ph.D.,
Charlotte S. Huck Professor of Children's Literature,
The Ohio State University, and
CHRISTINA COLÓN, Ph.D.,
Curator of Curriculum Development and Evaluation,
The New York Botanical Garden,
for their assistance in the preparation of this book.

First published in the UK by HarperCollins Children's Books in 2011
1 3 5 7 9 10 8 6 4 2
ISBN: 978-0-00-743307-0

Printed and bound in Hong Kong

I CAN NAME 50 TREES TODAY!

by Bonnie Worth

illustrated by Aristides Ruiz and Joe Mathieu

The Cat in the Hat's Learning Library®

HarperCollins *Children's Books*

I'm the Cat in the Hat
and I want you to please
take a few moments
to look at the trees!

If you pay close attention,
you might get to exclaim,

"There are 50 trees
I bet I can name!"

A tree is a plant
with a stem made of wood.
Do you know what a stem is?
A trunk! Very good.
Some trees grow to 10
or to 20 feet high.
Some grow till their tops
scrape the clouds in the sky.

98 FT.

PECAN

DEVIL'S
WALKING
STICK

30 FT.

10 FT.

FLOWERING DOGWOOD

A cypress in Mexico
that we have found
has a trunk more than
117 feet round!

BALD CYPRESS

A tree in Australia,
the land that's down under,
stands 492 feet tall—
oh my, what a wonder!

EUCALYPTUS

The branches grow upward.
The roots they grow down.
The branches and leaves
are what we call the crown.

Some crowns are like cones
(like this cute little fella).

AMERICAN HOLLY

SUGAR MAPLE

Some crowns match the shape
of my nifty umbrella.

AMERICAN ELM

WEEPING WILLOW

Some, like this willow,
droop down to the ground.

Some, like this apple tree,
are nearly round.

APPLE

WHITE OAK

I'd say this white oak is
as wide as it's tall,
while this pine doesn't have
low branches at all.

RED PINE

11

JAPANESE MAPLE

Let's look at the roots.
We will speak of them first.
They hold the tree up and
they help quench its thirst.

They draw water up
and, science has found,
they even draw minerals
out of the ground.

WILD FIG

OIL RIG

Nearly 400 feet deep
grow the roots of this fig.
That's almost as deep
as this oil-drilling rig.

BRANCHES

SHOOTS

LEAVES

The trunk and the branches,
the leaves and the shoots,
bring water and minerals
up from the roots.
The leaves then pull off
one tree-mendous feat.
They whip up the food
that the tree needs to eat.

SIBERIAN ELM

They mix water up
with rays from the sun,
add carbon dioxide and
when the leaf's done . . .
it gives off the oxygen
we need to survive.
(It's a gift from the trees
that keeps us alive.)

Here's a fast grower
(this will surely amaze ya).
Over one inch each day
this tree grows in Malaysia!

While way up in Canada
a four-inch slowpoke
is 155—
I tell you no joke!

ALBIZIA
FALCATA

ATLANTIC
WHITE CEDAR

Some leaves are so simple—
one leaf to each stem.
While others have
leaflets growing on them.

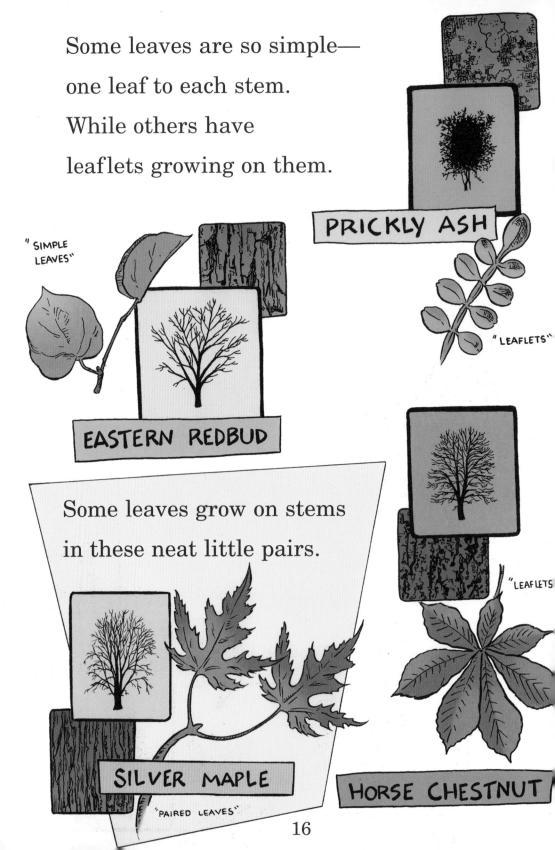

PRICKLY ASH

" SIMPLE
LEAVES"

" LEAFLETS"

EASTERN REDBUD

Some leaves grow on stems
in these neat little pairs.

"LEAFLETS

SILVER MAPLE

"PAIRED LEAVES"

HORSE CHESTNUT

16

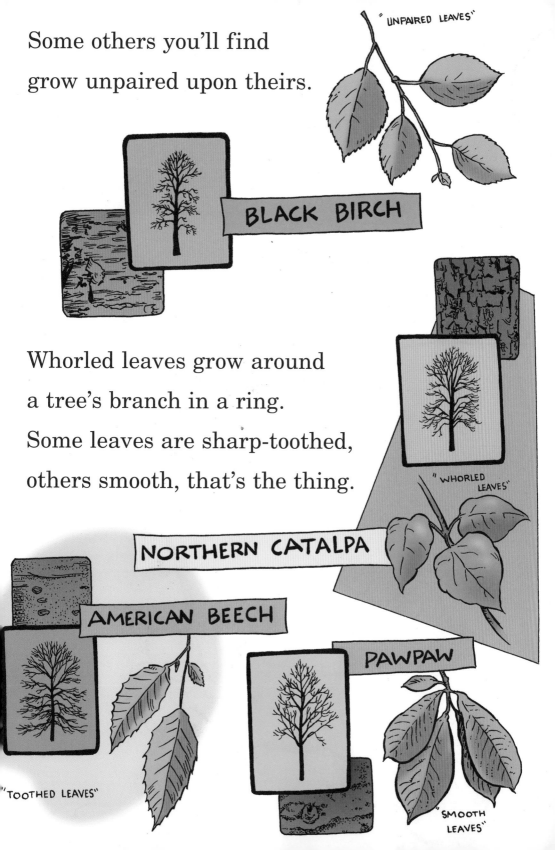

Some others you'll find
grow unpaired upon theirs.

"UNPAIRED LEAVES"

BLACK BIRCH

Whorled leaves grow around
a tree's branch in a ring.
Some leaves are sharp-toothed,
others smooth, that's the thing.

"WHORLED LEAVES"

NORTHERN CATALPA

AMERICAN BEECH

PAWPAW

"TOOTHED LEAVES"

"SMOOTH LEAVES"

Like your ears, some have lobes,
which means that they are
shaped a lot like your hand,
or a mitten, or star.

SWEET GUM

SASSAFRAS

FIELD MAPLE

19

Bark does for a tree
what your skin does for you:
stops the weather, the bugs,
and the germs getting through.

REDWOOD

The bark of the redwood,
you have to admire,
is two whole feet thick
and protects it from fire.

THING 1

20

The bark of this tree
is what has made it famous.
Shagbark hickory is what
this shaggy tree's name is.

SHAGBARK HICKORY

A neat trick a friend of mine
just showed to me
is to find out the age
of a once-living tree.

A new ring is added
with each living year.
Let's count up the rings
in this stump over here.

A year that has rain
leaves a ring that is thick.
This thin ring means drought
(or our poor tree was sick).

We've counted and we'll
share our answer with you.
It's 67—
did you find this was true?

SAPWOOD

HEARTWOOD

BARK

OLDEST-KNOWN
LIVING TREE

The oldest tree ever
(and this one is fine)
might be 4,700 years old—
a bristlecone pine.

BRISTLECONE PINE

CAVE
THING
2

There are all types of trees.
But of course you knew that.
One has needle-shaped leaves
or scales that are flat.
Its seeds come in pinecones,
so let's be exact
and say it's a conifer—
yes, that's a fact.

NEEDLE-LEAFED TREES

LARCH

WHITE PINE

SPRUCE

HEMLOCK

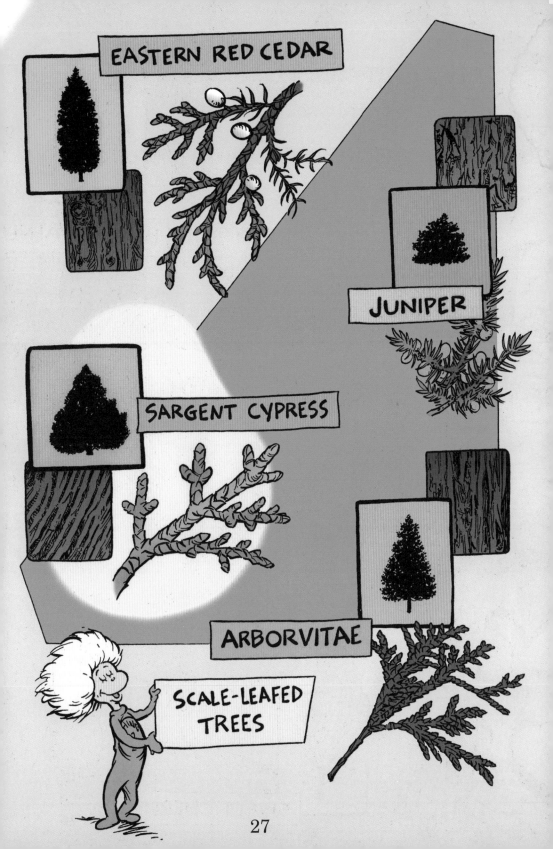

EASTERN RED CEDAR

JUNIPER

SARGENT CYPRESS

ARBORVITAE

SCALE-LEAFED TREES

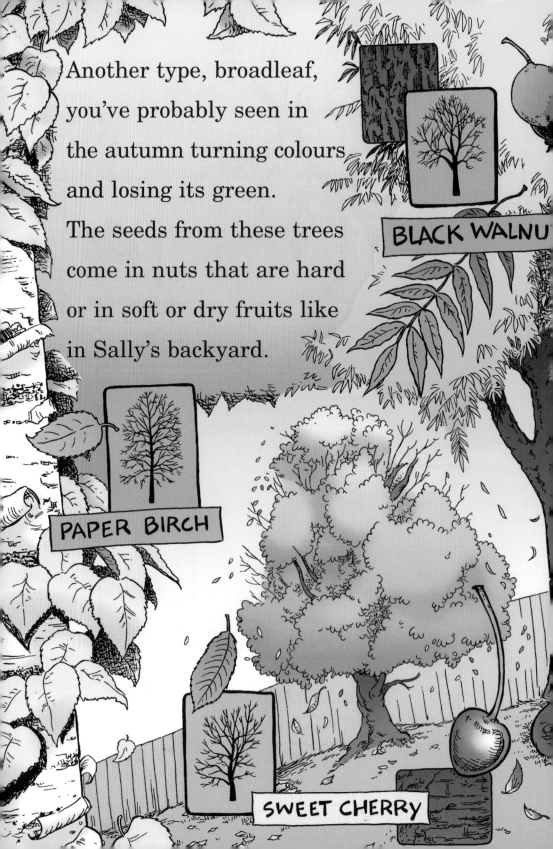

Another type, broadleaf,
you've probably seen in
the autumn turning colours
and losing its green.
The seeds from these trees
come in nuts that are hard
or in soft or dry fruits like
in Sally's backyard.

BLACK WALNU

PAPER BIRCH

SWEET CHERRY

RED MAPLE

"MAPLE FRUIT"

And then there are palms.
They grow where it's warm,
with leaves like a feather
or fan-like in form.

COCO-DE-MER

The world's largest seed,
from the coco-de-mer,
weighs 50 whole pounds.
Things, you'd better beware!

ROYAL PALM

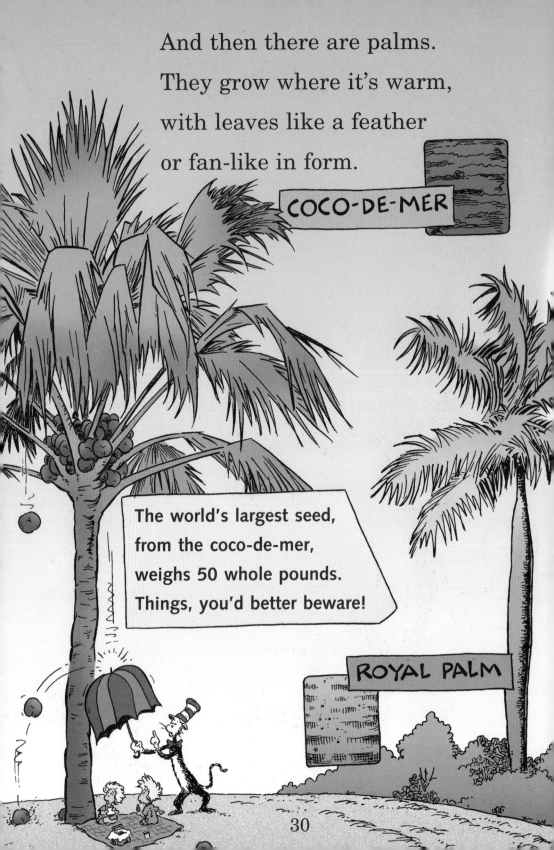

30

Forget not the lily trees,
lovely to see.
Like this king of the desert,
the Joshua tree.

JOSHUA TREE

If you ever get burned,
then you had better go
get the leaf of the yucca
that we call aloe.

YUCCA

The tree fern is oldest
and, what is more,
it doesn't have seeds.
Instead, it has spores.

The tree fern fares better
in much warmer weather.
This tree's rather short
with a leaf like a feather.

TREE
FERN

SPORES

The cycad is old
and, for what it is worth,
there were cycads when
dinosaurs once roamed the earth.
It looks like a palm,
but a palm it is not.
How long is its cone?
Three feet long! That's a lot!

SOUTH
AFRICAN
CYCAD

CONE

The tree called the ginkgo,
we've saved for the last.
The first one grew 250
million years in the past!

GINKGO

One thing that I think
you should know about ginkgo—
its fruit doesn't smell good.
In fact, it smells stinko!

Get yourself a blank book
to press leaves that you find.
Glue them onto the pages.
Your mother won't mind!

Note the tree's bark
and the shape of the crown.
Note the shape of the leaves
and then write it all down.

Take a look at this book
or get a tree guide.
Match up your leaves
to the pictures inside.

MEDIUM-SIZED to
LARGE TREE.
OPEN
SPREADING
CROWN

BLACK OAK

SHINY GREEN
ABOVE

YELLOW-
GREEN

BROWN

UNDER

LOBED LEAVES

ACORN

ARK-
REY & SMOOTH-
coming blackish
hick and rough
DEEPLY FURROWED
RIDGES

Write down the tree names
and learn them by heart.
This book contains 50
and that's a great start.

37

Knowing trees' names,
my dear miss and dear mister,
is like knowing the name of
your brother or sister.

We can't have enough of these
wonderful trees.

So when you see bare spots . . .

. . . go plant a tree, please!

GLOSSARY

Drought: A time during which no rain falls, which is difficult for plants and animals.

Germs: Tiny living things, too small to see with the naked eye, that can cause sickness or disease.

Heartwood: The innermost part of the trunk of a tree, which no longer carries sap.

Lobes: Curved edges (such as on leaves) that stick out.

Minerals: Natural substances found in the ground that plants absorb to help them grow strong and big.

Quench: To bring to an end—as in to quench a thirst by taking a drink.

Sapwood: The soft, living part of the trunk of a tree which lies between the inner bark and the heartwood.

Spores: Tiny grains given off by some plants or trees that make new plants.

Whorled: Spiraling out from a central point.

INDEX